# EXTREME CAREERS

# STUNT PERFORMERS
## Life Before the Camera

Chérie Turner

rosen central
*the rosen publishing group's*

Published in 2001, 2005 by The Rosen Publishing Group, Inc.
29 East 21st Street, New York, NY 10010

Copyright © 2001, 2005 by The Rosen Publishing Group, Inc.

**Revised Edition**

All rights reserved. No part of this book may be reproduced in any form without permission in writing from the publisher, except by a reviewer.

### Library of Congress Cataloging-in-Publication Data

Turner, Chérie.
Stunt performers: life before the camera/by Chérie Turner
    p. cm.—(Extreme careers)
Includes bibliographical references.
ISBN: 978-1-4358-3740-9
1. Stunt performers—Vocational guidance—Juvenile literature.
I. Title. II. Series.
PN1995.9.S7 T87 2001
791.43'029'8—dc21

                                                                                                            00-011752

*Manufactured in the United States of America*

# Contents

| | | |
|---|---|---|
| | A Dangerous Business | 4 |
| 1 | Life as a Stunt Performer | 8 |
| 2 | Types of Stunts | 16 |
| 3 | The Business of Stunt Performing | 37 |
| 4 | The Big Picture | 47 |
| | Glossary | 54 |
| | For More Information | 56 |
| | For Further Reading | 59 |
| | Index | 61 |

# A Dangerous Business

"Quiet on the set! Lights! Camera! Action!" Six cameras with film rolling keep their lenses focused on a sixth-floor window—waiting for the action to happen. Up on that floor, ninety feet above the ground, a stunt support crew sets a man on fire. The burning man turns toward the window and takes off running at full speed. Fully engulfed in flames and almost blind to where he can go because it is dark outside, he breaks through the window and falls into the night. On the ground, a large air bag and another support crew waits for him. He hits the air bag with a mighty force. The support crew runs in quickly to put out the flames. The stuntman emerges from the air bag, safe and sound. "That's a wrap! Good job, everybody!"

## A Dangerous Business

This may seem like something you see only in the movies, and it is. For the people who actually perform these physically demanding acts of danger, however, it's all in a day's work. These people (like Shane "Torch" Anderson, who performed the previously described stunt, or "gag," as it is called in the film industry) are stunt performers. It is their job to take over when the action in a movie is too dangerous for the actor playing the role. When a stunt performer fills in for an actor, it is called being a double, or doubling. However, sometimes stunt performers get their own roles in movies because they are able to perform amazing stunts and also act.

Stunt performers have been around since the days of Shakespeare in the 1500s. Back then, if you were an actor, it helped if you also knew how to perform stunts. Sword fights were especially popular. To be convincing, actors who played these parts had to be expert swordsmen and make the combat look real without anyone actually getting hurt. Many of the most popular actors of that time were some of the best sword fighters in England.

The need for actors to be stunt performers as well didn't change much when people started making

## Stunt Performers: Life Before the Camera

movies. Early films were silent films, which means that they had no sound. They had to have a lot of action to keep the audience entertained. Instead of being sword fighters, many early film actors were talented rodeo or circus performers because action with horses was very popular.

When "talkies," or films with sound, were created, there was less action and more dialogue. Filmmakers needed people who were skilled at acting, not just performing stunts. Many actors who starred in early films were better at stunt performing than acting. However, people who could act often could not perform

Like Harold Lloyd (pictured here), many of the actors and actresses in early films were required to be skilled stuntpeople.

## A Dangerous Business

stunts. A need developed for a professional who could double for the actor. The profession of stunt performing was born. Today, stunt performing is its own career, and the people who do it are stunt specialists. Although many stunt performers are also actors, most are only involved in the stunt aspect of movies and other projects, such as music videos, video games, television programs, and theme parks. They work to create and perform the most fantastic action scenes possible.

# Life as a Stunt Performer

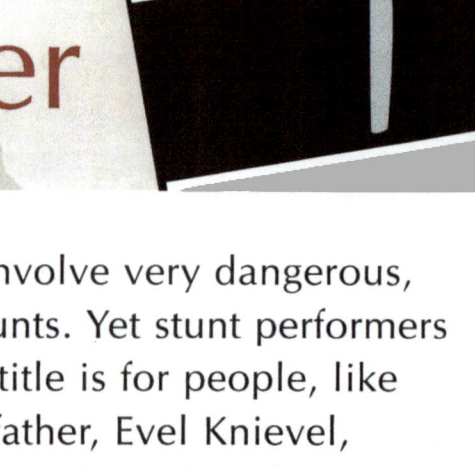

Stunt performing can involve very dangerous, often life-threatening, stunts. Yet stunt performers are not daredevils. That title is for people, like Robbie Knievel and his father, Evel Knievel, whose primary goal is to perform the most daring stunts possible.

A stunt performer, on the other hand, performs a specific, physically challenging act that is requested by a director. Though stunt performers do test their personal limits, this is not their primary goal. Their goal is to complete the requested action, have it recorded on film, and escape from the stunt injury-free, so they can be ready for the next job that comes along.

Life as a Stunt Performer

# What the Job Requires

Stuntpeople are asked to perform any number of different stunts, from high falls to fight scenes to car chases. For this reason, most stunt performers try to be versatile, or able to do as many types of stunts as possible. In order to be versatile, performers must be very athletic and fit. They must also be able to face new challenges with confidence, which requires them to be mentally tough. Finally, they must be able to work well with other people and be able to take direction well.

# Physical Demands

Stunt performing is a physically demanding job. Because of this, stunt performers must be strong and agile, or able to move quickly and gracefully. They must also be very physically coordinated. This means being able to have precise control over their muscles and body movements. Being physically fit not only prepares stunt performers to do stunts, it also helps them to reduce the chance of injuries.

Martial arts training can teach you many skills needed for stunt work, including coordination, flexibility, and the ability to calm the mind.

## Life as a Stunt Performer

Most people who are stunt performers love sports and enjoy pushing their physical limits. Some sports that are popular among stunt performers are motocross, mountain bike riding, snowboarding, in-line skating, rock climbing, scuba diving, horseback riding, gymnastics, and trampolining. Many stuntpeople are also skilled in martial arts. As stunt man and author Mark Aisbett points out in his book, *So You Wanna Be a Stunt Man*, "Skills you learn in martial arts which translate to stunt work are balance, timing, coordination, taking direction, focus, discipline, flexibility, and, most importantly, the ability to calm one's mind." These activities help a performer stay fit and help keep the performer's skills sharp so he or she can perform at a moment's notice.

## Mental Toughness

Stunt performers must be willing to put themselves in physically challenging situations. Most of the work they do is very dangerous. They must be able to face these situations with a clear mind and stay focused and calm. They must master fear. This may be one of the toughest parts of being a stunt performer. Even if they can physically do the stunt, if

Amy Lyndon *(right)* poses with her stunt double, Lynn Salvatori, on the set of the television series *Freddie's Nightmare*.

they lose concentration or are scared, they can put themselves in great danger.

In order to be certain that they will be mentally prepared, stunt performers practice a number of different mental exercises. Some stunt performers meditate and practice breathing exercises to help clear their mind and feel calm and controlled. Others may practice visualization. This means imagining a stunt over and over in their mind. This mental preparation works well for up-and-coming stuntwoman Minerva Adams, who says, "If I can see it [in my head], I can do it."

## Teamwork

When we think of stunt performers, we may think only about the part of the job that requires them to be fearless and do amazing stunts. What we forget is that someone else plans that stunt. That person is called a stunt coordinator. The stunt performer has to do the stunt to the exact specifications he or she is given. They are also part of a much larger crew of people who all work together to produce the stunt and the film. No one wants to work with someone who is difficult, especially on a movie set where days are long and the pressure to get the action perfect can be high.

## Acting

Stunt performers are also actors. When they are doubling for the actor who is really playing the part, they must convince the audience that they are that actor. Although they probably won't say a line, and you certainly won't see their face, they still need to move like the actor and must act in a way that fits in with the other action in the film.

## Stunt Performers: Life Before the Camera

Other times, a stunt performer will be hired to play a character because that role primarily requires someone who can perform stunts. These are usually smaller parts. However, people like Jackie Chan, Chuck Norris, and Jean-Claude Van Damme have made entire careers out of combining their stunt performing talents with acting.

Jackie Chan jumps from a moving train in the movie *Shanghai Moon*. He has made a career out of combining his stunt performing talents with acting.

## Life as a Stunt Performer

# Ready for Action

Bringing together all of the elements necessary to become a successful stunt performer takes time. Not surprisingly, many people who get into the business have been performers or competitive athletes for years. Many stunt performers grew up performing in the circus or rodeo. Others, however, just set out to pursue the profession and put in the hard work and training that is required to do the job. Fit, skilled, mentally tough, and able to fall into character, stunt performers are ready to face the various challenges that the profession demands.

# Types of Stunts

There are many types of stunts, or gags, that are regularly used in films and television. The following are some of the most common types of gags that stunt performers train themselves to do.

## High Falls

High falls are relatively common, but they can be very dangerous. For example, during the filming of *A Vampire in Brooklyn*, stunt performer Sonja Davis suffered massive head injuries from a forty-five-foot fall. She died eleven days later. Many other stuntpeople have died doing this type of gag. The most important

## Types of Stunts

part of a high fall for a stunt performer is the landing. To avoid injury, he or she must fall on his or her back. The performer can execute any action that the director asks for while in the air, such as flailing arms or tumbling around and around, but to make sure that the stunt ends safely, he or she always tries to land front side up.

Depending on the height of the fall, the performer will land on different types of surfaces. For

Although they are relatively common, high falls are dangerous and can result in the injury or death of a stunt performer if not done properly.

This nine-foot-deep air bag was used to cushion a sixty-one-foot fall, performed by stuntwoman Lynn Salvatori in the film *Pure Luck*.

## Types of Stunts

short falls, performers usually use a mat (like you might find in gym class) or stacks of empty cardboard boxes with the corners folded in, or a combination of these items stacked on top of each other. For high falls, stunt performers use an air bag. You may have seen these before. They are large, air-filled bags that are supportive but that give way when the performer lands. Though performers make it look easy to hit such a large target, remember, it looks a lot smaller when they are looking down on it from so high above the ground. Martin Grace, a stunt man who worked on many of the early James Bond movies, describes in the book *Burns, Falls, and Crashes: Interviews with Movie Stunt Performers* what the air bag looks like from the vantage point of the jumper: "I took a photograph looking down on [the air bag] from a hundred feet up. You can see this little rig just between my legs, looking like a small postage stamp." Sometimes—as in the stunt described at the beginning of the book—the performer may not even see the bag when he or she is making the jump. In those cases, the stunt performer must study the stunt well and remember where the bag is before he or she starts the gag.

A stuntperson performing a burn requires various types of protection, such as fireproof gel, a Nomex suit, and a fire suit. The stuntman pictured here is performing a burn at a stuntperson awards show.

Types of Stunts

# Burns

Burns are often considered the most dangerous stunts because fire is always unpredictable. Burns are also dangerous because injuries can happen very quickly and, unlike broken bones or muscle strains, burns are permanent. Five seconds can be the difference between no injuries and severe, even life-threatening, damage. When a stunt performer does a burn, it is either a partial (on one part of the body) or a full (over the entire body) burn.

To perform a burn, a stunt performer must first cover the area of his or her body that will be set on fire with a fireproof gel. Often, he or she will put on a suit that looks like long underwear, called a Nomex suit. Nomex suits have special fibers in them that expand when heated. The big fibers shield the skin from burns. This suit is also often soaked in the fireproof gel. Over the Nomex suit, the stunt performer wears a fire suit, very much like the ones worn by race car drivers, which gives further protection against getting burned. Then, over that, he or she wears the costume. If the scene allows it, the stunt performer

## Stunt Performers: Life Before the Camera

may also wear a helmet with a thick face shield. Over this, a rubber costume mask is worn to make the performer look like a real person. In a full burn or a partial that will occur around the face, the stunt performer will receive oxygen from a tank he or she carries. On top of all of that, something flammable—which acts as a fuel for the fire—like rubber cement or contact cement, is put where the burn is supposed to happen. Then the performer is set on fire. Even with all of the protective gear and gel, a stunt performer is safe for no more than thirty seconds. If the fire is not extinguished within this time period, not only will the stunt performer get burned, he or she might not be able to breathe!

What if the action calls for the stunt performer not to be fully clothed? Torch Anderson faced this challenge when he was asked to perform a full body burn in shorts! To complete this stunt, he worked with people from a university to develop a special fuel that would burn at a lower temperature than the kind stunt performers normally use. He also had to find a way to breathe. Fire uses oxygen, and in a full body burn, fire would be all around his face. There would be no oxygen for him to breathe.

## Types of Stunts

Also, breathing in hot flames would burn his mouth and lungs, which could cause death. He could not use an oxygen tank because it would be seen on film. What did he do? Anderson put a wet sponge in his mouth. The heat from the fire turned the water in the sponge into steam. The steam had oxygen in it that he could breathe.

Anderson's burn was a success. With all of this careful planning, Anderson burned for the camera for a full twelve seconds! He did not suffer any injuries.

Although transfers are some of the most dangerous stunts, they are performed with almost no safety measures, aside from padding.

The movie *Lethal Weapon* makes good use of the crash-filled stunt driving that fans of action movies love.

# Transfers

Many of the most exciting stunts involve a performer moving from one moving object to another, such as from a motorcycle to a moving train. This type of stunt is called a transfer. These stunts are some of the oldest and most dangerous known to the stunt profession. Aside from padding, there are almost no safety measures that can be taken to make these gags safer. These gags require good timing, a confident mind, and a lot of practice. One wrong move and the stunt performer is sure to be badly injured.

# Stunt Driving

A car chase filled with crashes, rolls, and fast driving is a favorite among audiences. But even something as seemingly simple as a 360-degree turn in which the car spins all the way around, or a roll, takes a great deal of experience and practice. There are over five schools in the United States that specialize in teaching stunt driving, but many people learn stunts on their own or are taught by other stunt performers.

   A car that is used in stunt scenes is specially set up so that it is as safe as possible. Handles and

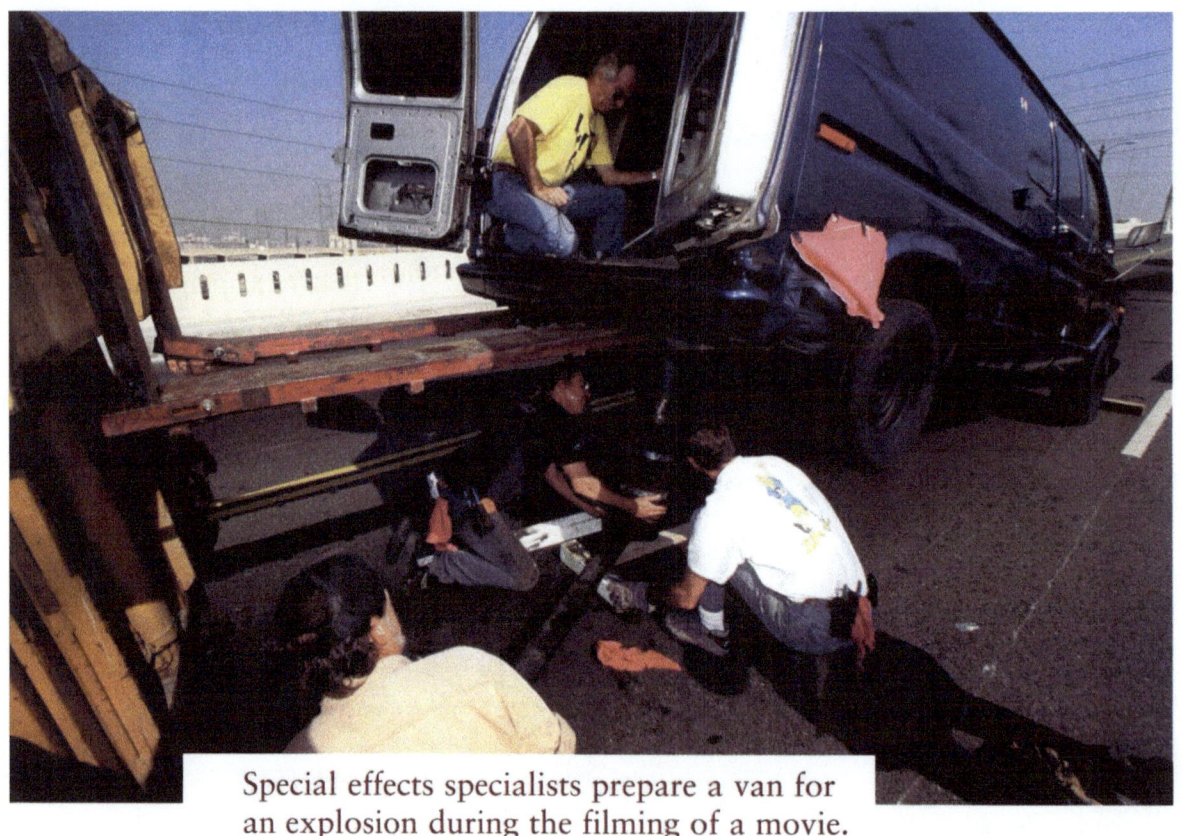
Special effects specialists prepare a van for an explosion during the filming of a movie.

anything else that stick out are removed so that the stunt performer will not be poked or impaled. The car is reinforced so that the stuntperson will not get smashed or trapped inside. The regular gas tank may even be removed and replaced with a smaller, sturdier tank that is less likely to catch on fire or blow up. The driver usually wears a full set of pads and a helmet.

Even with all of these safety precautions, stunt drivers do get injured. If the timing of a stunt is off

## Types of Stunts

by even less than a second, a stunt performer can suffer severe injuries.

# Fight Scenes

Hand-to-hand combat is featured in many action movies. How many times does the final scene come down to the good guy and the bad guy duking it out? And who doesn't love to see what amazingly innovative

Vehicles that are used in stunt scenes are specially set up so that they are as safe as possible.

Lynn Salvatori gets help strapping on special explosives for a stunt illusion.

fight sequences Jackie Chan will think up next to wow the audience?

Though fight scenes look very spontaneous and dramatic, they are actually very well planned and choreographed. The performers and others involved in the creation of a fight scene choreograph every movement, down to each kick, fall, and punch. They create a routine that makes punches and blows look real and painful. Camera angles, stage fighting techniques—in which people make fake

## Types of Stunts

fighting look real—and the various skills of the stunt performers are used to treat the audience to the most fantastic fight scenes possible.

## Stunt Illusions

Although a lot of the action on screen really does take place, much of what we see is fake or an illusion. These illusions make the stunts either safer for

You can tell by Lynn Salvatori's smile that she is not hurt. She is pleased with the outcome of the stunt illusion.

## Stunt Performers: Life Before the Camera

the stuntperson or appear more real to the audience. Some of the most common illusions are explosions, gunshots, blood, and breaking glass and furniture.

# Explosions and Gunshots

Ever wonder how an actor or an actress really goes flying backward when he or she has been hit by a bullet in a movie? The person was not really shot, so how's it done? What about when there is an explosion and the person is thrown through the air? How is it that one second he or she is standing still and the next the person is flying through the air?

To make these scenes appear real, stunt performers rely on different devices. To make it look like someone is flying through the air, either a mini-trampoline or an air ram—a platform that launches the stunt performer into the air—is used. The advantage of the air ram is that the stunt performer can be sent flying from a standing position or in the midst of running, as might be called for in a battle scene in which a person steps on a land mine.

Another device that is used in stunt performing is called a ratchet. Oftentimes, a ratchet is used to

Stunt performer Ritchie Copenhaver practices with a ratchet.

make a person look as if he or she has been shot. This device is made up of a harness that the performer wears, which is attached to a cable. When the stunt performer is "shot," the cable is pulled by a "puller" very quickly, giving the illusion that the person is reacting to the force of a bullet. Though it may seem like the machine does all of the work in this type of stunt, it is actually a very physically demanding stunt. The performer must be able to make himself or herself very relaxed. This

## Stunt Performers: Life Before the Camera

requires great concentration and a calm mind. Otherwise, the person could end up with torn muscles, whiplash, or other serious injuries.

# Breaking Up

When a stunt performer is thrown through a window, he or she is not breaking real glass. Instead, candy glass, also called breakaway glass, is used. Candy glass got its name a long time ago when it was made out of sugar and water. Today, a type of plastic that shatters dramatically on impact is used. The James Bond movie *Die Another Day* used over six tons of SMASH! plastic glass in its arctic scenes.

When chairs or other furniture are broken over someone's head in a film, they are made out of a soft wood called balsa wood. Also, nails are never used in furniture that is going to be used in a stunt.

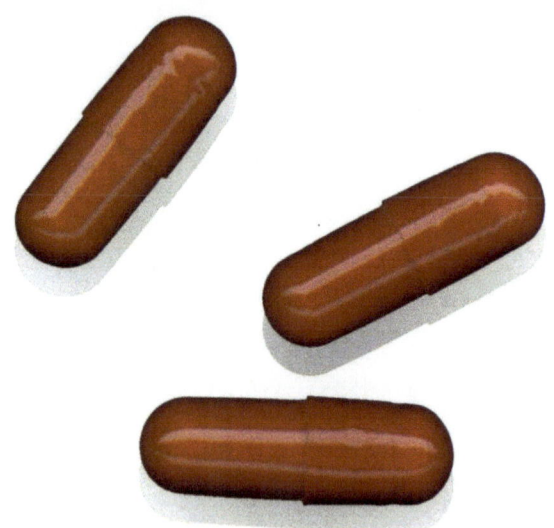

Actors bite down on small "blood" capsules to mimic bleeding from the mouth.

## Types of Stunts

Instead the furniture is held together with glue. Stunt and film furniture is called prop furniture.

# Blood

When actors are hit by a bullet or punched in the face, it is not real blood that stains their clothing. Instead, what you see is either a combination of sugar water, corn syrup, and food coloring, or is made up of that mixture with some additional chemicals added to it. (In the early days of film, they actually used ketchup.) There are a variety of different types of fake blood, depending on what the action calls for. For example, some "blood" is runny while other "blood" is thick or clots.

A small explosive device called a squib is sometimes used to release red liquid hidden in the actor's clothing to produce "blood."

There are several different ways that blood may be used in a stunt scene. If someone is getting shot, the "blood" may be inside pellets that are shot from a fake gun in much the same way a paint gun shoots paint

# The Real Deal

Many stunts today use camera tricks, props, stunt skills, or computer technology to make action that does not actually happen appear real on film. For example, in fight scenes, no one actually gets punched. When someone is thrown through a window, the person is not breaking through real glass. This was not always the case.

When people first started performing stunts, much of the action was real. In her book *Movie Stunts and the People Who Do Them*, Gloria D. Miklowitz recalls, "In the early days, fight scenes were the real thing. Men really hit each other. Chairs were thrown; real glass windows, broken."

Not only was the action real, it was unplanned. As author David Jon Wiener describes in the book *Burns, Falls, and Crashes: Interviews with Movie Stunt Performers*, "In the old days, stunt fights were totally unplanned; two men simply started swinging when the director shouted 'Action' and didn't stop until they heard 'Cut.' " Wiener even recalls a few instances in which real bullets were used! In the same book, stuntwoman Polly Burson recalls times when real arrows were sent flying across the set!

balls. They splatter when they hit the stuntperson. Other times, there is a packet of the red liquid hidden in the actor's clothing and attached to a squib—a small explosive device—which is set off when the action happens. If an actor has to bleed from the mouth, a small capsule, much like a vitamin pill, is kept in the performer's mouth, and he or she bites on it to get the "blood" to come out.

# No Two Stunts Are the Same

One of the most challenging aspects of stunt performing is the fact that stunts almost always come with a twist. Perhaps a director wants a motorcycle to jump over a car. That's not too challenging, right? True, if that's all that is required. But say, in this stunt, you are indoors, the ceiling is low, there is an explosion under the motorcycle while it travels through the air, and there is a wall on the other side of the car that is only ten feet away. You must first consider the height of the space to be sure you don't crash into the ceiling. Then you must consider what is going to happen to the motorcycle when the explosion goes off. Then

## Stunt Performers: Life Before the Camera

you must figure out the length of the jump needed to clear the car and figure out your speed. Finally, you must figure out how to land and not hit the wall.

One of the biggest challenges that stunt performers face is that they must do a stunt within the very specific guidelines of the director. This is where planning and experience become very important. Stunts must be planned very carefully. Every detail must be considered, and those details change with each stunt. The smallest detail overlooked or mistake can mean disaster. Not only will the director not get the film footage he or she needs, but the stunt performer could be badly injured or even killed.

# More Than Just Stunts

The main job of a stunt performer is to perform daring actions like the burns, falls, and car chases that we talked about in this chapter. But to be successful in this profession, stunt performers must do more than just perform stunts. In order to get a job, a stunt performer must be a part of the filmmaking business.

# The Business of Stunt Performing

Successful stunt performers work not just to do stunts but also to get those stunts captured on film. They must be a part of the film industry. One thing this means is that they must live in an area where films are made. "Location is vital," says the letter that is sent to prospective stunt performers from the Stuntmen's Association of Motion Pictures. "You must live in the Los Angeles area if you want to pursue this [stunt performer] career." Although this is excellent industry advice, there are other areas, such as New York City, North Carolina, and Florida, where stunt performers may find work. There is also a growing amount of film work being done in the bigger cities in Canada, such as Toronto, Vancouver, and Montreal.

A film crew shoots the fire from a stunt car that was dropped twenty feet from a parking structure in downtown Los Angeles in 1997.

## The Business of Stunt Performing

Location is just one thing that must be considered by those who make their career in stunt performing. This chapter will discuss in greater detail some of the other important elements that stuntpeople must deal with as performers in the film industry.

# Competition

The profession of stunt performing is very competitive. According to *USA Today*'s Ann Oldenburg, more than 6,000 stunt performers are registered with the Screen Actors Guild. Less than 1,000 of these performers earned more than $25,000 in the year 2002. At the same time, a small group of 200 to 300 stunt performers have made yearly salaries ranging from $40,000 to $700,000. This means competition is tight.

One of the reasons that this profession is so competitive is because stunt performers can make a lot of money. Performers who are part of the Screen Actors Guild union (unions will be discussed in greater detail later in this chapter) receive just over $600 simply for being on the set. They then earn an additional amount, called an adjustment, per stunt. The amount of the adjustment depends on the amount of risk and

## Stunt Performers: Life Before the Camera

the complexity of the stunt. A low-risk stunt may earn a performer a few hundred dollars, while a risky stunt may be worth several thousand.

Even though stunt performers can make a lot of money when they work, competition can keep those opportunities scarce. Many who are breaking into the profession suffer hard times. In *Burns, Falls, and Crashes: Interviews with Movie Stunt Performers*, stunt man John Cade recalls a time when he lived off a case of canned peas that a neighbor had given him because he was broke. It can take years before a performer makes enough money to live well. According to the Stuntmen's Association of Motion Pictures, "you must be prepared to spend approximately five to eight years becoming established."

Even those who have been in the business a long time may see many days without work. There are never any guarantees that jobs will come your way on a regular basis. According to many people who have been in the business for a long time, it is getting more and more competitive. To be a successful stunt performer, a person has to really want the job and always be looking for the next gag. It has to be his or her number one priority in life.

### The Business of Stunt Performing

## Growing Demand

Despite the great amount of competition and the fact that computer technology is now able to create some action sequences without the use of stunt performers, it looks as if there will be a continuing need for people who perform stunts. According the the U.S. Bureau of Labor Statistics, the film industry will grow at a rate of 31 percent between 2002 and 2012. This means more jobs, more projects, and more work opportunities. Stunt work is also expanding into new areas. Cable television projects and music videos are becoming more and more action-oriented. Stunt performers are also used in the creation of many video games.

## "It's Who You Know"

You have likely heard this phrase used when people talk about getting hired for a job. This is especially true in the world of stunt performing. People usually enjoy working with others whom they know and trust. Directors want to know that the person they hire to do

Many new stunt performers will get other types of jobs on a film set so they can be around people who might hire them to do stunt work.

a stunt is going to do the job right. This is important because many stunts can be performed only one time, and they are very dangerous. Also, because of the great amount of competition, those in the stunt community work to keep themselves and their fellow stunt friends employed. They are not always so welcoming to those just starting out.

So how do stunt performers get into the business? Some people are born into it, such as Sean Skene, whose father has over fifty movie credits. Sean's uncle

## The Business of Stunt Performing

is also a stunt performer. People like Sean have a relative who is in the business. They grow up being friends with all the right people. Other people get lucky and meet and develop a friendship with someone who works in movies. Others simply work extra hard to make sure that they get to know those key people. This is called networking. Many new stunt performers will get other types of jobs on a film set, like working as an extra, so they can be around and meet the people who might hire them to do stunt work. Or sometimes a stunt performer may find out where filming is going to take place, find the stunt coordinator (the person who plans stunts and hires stuntpeople), and give that person his or her resumes.

A stunt performer must be prepared to work very hard to get into the world of film. It is not an easy or kind business. But if a stuntperson wants to be in the profession badly enough, there are ways to break in.

# Agencies and Unions

Stunt performers who work in film and television must belong to a union. In the United States, stunt performers

## Stunt Performers: Life Before the Camera

are in the same union that actors and actresses are in: the Screen Actors Guild (SAG). Stunt performers in Canada usually join the Alliance of Canadian Cinema, Television, and Radio Artists (ACTRA).

Unlike actors, however, stunt performers are not represented by agents (unless they also want to pursue acting), and they do not audition for gags. Instead, they become part of an agency, such as the Stuntmen's Association of Motion Pictures or the United Stuntwomen's Association. These agencies work to

The stunt coordinator *(left)*, the safety technician taking measurements and checking for rocks, and the cowboy holding a gun are all stunt professionals.

make sure that their members work on the best paying, most prestigious projects. Stunt performers also get hired based on their experience and reputation. However, there is a catch. To become a member of an agency, a performer must be invited to join, and this can take years. This is often one of the most difficult steps on the way to breaking into the stunt performing business.

# Jobs Related to Stunt Performing

There are several different types of jobs in the film industry that a stunt performer can pursue besides performing stunts. Generally, they require a person to have several years of stunt performing experience behind him or her.

## Rigger

A rigger is the person who sets up the equipment for the stunt. Many people who do this job have experience in rock climbing. They understand how to safely rig harnesses and ropes. The key here is safety. Riggers

### Stunt Performers: Life Before the Camera

have to be very detail-oriented. The stunt performer relies on the rigger to set everything up so that the stunt will go off as safely as possible.

## Stunt Coordinator

Just like the name implies, these people are responsible for figuring out how a stunt is going to happen. They work with both the director—who tells them what needs to happen—and the stunt performers to create action sequences. Stunt coordinators also hire the stunt performers, making them essential contacts for stunt performers who are networking.

## Second Unit Director

Second unit directors are responsible for filming anything that does not involve the stars. In relation to stunt performing, they are the people who are responsible for the action scenes. They often work with the stunt coordinator and the stunt performers to film action scenes.

# The Big Picture

Once a stunt performer is hired, the performer plans out and prepares for the stunt. Then the shoot-date or filming day comes. This is what it all leads up to: It's time to perform.

## Show Up and Get Ready

First, it is important that the stunt performer show up early so that he or she is certain to be ready when the director calls, "Action." Time is money on a film set, and the stunt performer doesn't want to keep anyone waiting.

If necessary, the stunt performer must go to wardrobe and get his or her costume. After

# One Shot Is All You Get — *The World According to Garp*

Experience and skill were two key ingredients used to pull off an amazing stunt for the movie *The World According to Garp*. The director wanted a pilot to fly an airplane into a house and have the front of the plane go through the roof but have the wings and tail sticking up out of the roof. Stunt man and experienced pilot James S. Appleby was called in to do the job. It took months of planning. A plane was specially constructed, and a house was specifically built for this stunt. The main planning for the plane had to do with what was (or was not) in the cockpit and what was to be done with the gas tank so that it would not explode during the crash. The challenge of building the house was to make it sturdy enough so that it would stay standing when the plane hit it, but not so sturdy that the pilot would be hurt when he crashed into it. The main concern for the pilot (aside from his life!) was to crash into the house at just the right speed so that the plane would not go through the house. Yet he had to fly fast enough to keep the plane in the air! So how did they do it?

    The house was built with hard woods except in the exact location on the roof where the plane was going to hit. This meant that the pilot had an area that was only

## The Big Picture

eight feet wide and eight feet high that he could safely hit. If he was off a foot in any direction, he risked severe injury and the shot would be ruined. The plane had a very small gas tank that was made to fall off and away from the plane if it was hit. Also, there was no control panel or front seat in the cockpit! They could not risk the possibility of the pilot hitting or being hit by anything in the plane.

How did Appleby know how fast he was going? He used his experience as a pilot to feel the speed of the plane. Remember, he had to fly at a specific speed. Too slow and the plane would not fly. Too fast and the plane would go through the house. Specifically, Appleby had to keep the plane flying faster than forty-seven miles per hour, but no more than fifty-two—without a speedometer! Finally, there was the issue of stopping the plane, which had to happen in just sixteen feet. To do this, they rigged the inside of the house with a net to catch the plane. There were also two telephone poles inside the house that the wings would hit that also helped to slow the plane.

With all this careful planning and the amazing flying skills of Appleby, the stunt went off without a problem and the image of the plane sticking out of the house became the one that was used to promote the film.

It is important for the stunt performer to go over the details of the stunt with the stunt coordinator.

wardrobe, it's time for hair and makeup. Once a stunt performer looks the part, it's time to physically and mentally prepare to do the stunt. In order to physically prepare for a stunt, a performer may need to stretch to warm up his or her body. This is especially true if the stunt is extremely challenging, like a martial arts fight.

## The Big Picture

Even more important than being physically prepared for a stunt is being mentally prepared. If stunt performers are afraid or not focused, they can put themselves and others in serious danger. Many performers spend some quiet time alone before they perform, going through some last minute visualization or quieting their minds with meditation. With many stunts, one take is all a stuntperson gets. He or she needs to be ready to give 110 percent.

Finally, it is important to check and double-check all the equipment that is going to be involved in the stunt. Even if someone else has already made sure everything is ready, it is the stunt performer who is at risk, so it is important that he or she checks things out. Remember, the smallest detail left unattended can lead to injury or disaster.

# At the End of the Day

Once a stunt performer is done with his or her stunt, it is never a bad idea to linger on the set. Oftentimes, other stunt opportunities come up. If a

Stuntman Tony Cecere prepares for a burn by soaking clothes in fire retardant gel.

stuntperson is hanging around, he or she may be asked to perform these additional gags.

When the day is done, the stunt performer must be certain to return his or her costume in good condition. It is also a good idea for a stunt performer to help clean up. This will help ensure that he or she is welcome on the next job. Once the final thank-yous and good-byes have been said, it is time to return home and start preparing for the next gag.

**The Big Picture**

# A Final Word About Being a Stunt Performer

Living the life of a stunt performer is as tough as it is rewarding. The work is challenging, dangerous, and often difficult to get. The pay can be great, but only if a stunt performer can get hired. Getting that first gag can take years of focused dedication, and there's no guarantee that a stunt performer will get hired for more work even if he or she does have experience. One thing is certain, though, stunt performers love what they do. For them, the job of burning, crashing, and falling compares to no other.

# Glossary

**air bag**  A safety device that catches a stunt performer when he or she performs a high fall.

**air ram**  A platform that launches a stunt performer into the air. It is often used in scenes where there are explosions.

**breakaway glass**  Special glass used for stunts. It is treated so it will break into small pieces instead of sharp and dangerous shards. It is also called candy glass.

**doubling**  Filling in for an actor or actress.

**high fall**  A type of stunt where a performer falls from a great distance and lands on an air bag to break his or her fall.

**prop furniture**  A type of furniture built specially to break apart. Prop furniture is often made of a light

# Glossary

wood called balsa wood and held together without the use of nails.

**ratchet**  A device made up of a cable and a harness, used to make people look like they are flying or reacting to a gunshot or an explosion.

**resumes**  A one-page summary of a person's experience and abilities.

**rigger**  The person responsible for setting up the equipment for a stunt.

**second unit director**  The director in charge of all filming that does not involve the star actors and actresses.

**squib**  A small explosive device often used to give the appearance of a gunshot. Also used with fake blood to make a person look as if he or she has been shot.

**stunt coordinator**  The person in charge of creating a stunt and figuring out how it will be performed. He or she is also responsible for hiring the stunt performers.

**transfer**  A type of stunt where a performer moves from one moving object to another, such as jumping from a car onto a train.

# For More Information

**Screen Actors Guild (SAG)**
5757 Wilshire Boulevard
Los Angeles, CA 90036-3600
(323) 954-1600
Web site: http://www.sag.org

**Stuntmen's Association of Motion Pictures**
10660 Riverside Drive, 2nd Floor, Suite E
Toluca Lake, CA 91602
(818) 766-4334
e-mail: info@stuntmen.com
Web site: http://www.stuntmen.com

**Stuntwomen's Association of Motion Pictures**
12457 Ventura Boulevard, Suite 208
Studio City, CA 91604
(818) 762-0907

## For More Information

e-mail: stuntwomen@stuntwomen.com
Web site: http://www.stuntwomen.com

### United Stuntmen's Association
2723 Saratoga Lane
Everett, WA 98203
(425) 290-9957
Web site: http://stuntschool.com

### United Stuntwomen's Association
P.O. Box 1483
Studio City, CA 91614
(323) 874-3584
e-mail: usa@usastunts.com
Web site: http://www.usastunts.com

# In Canada

### ACTRA (The Alliance of Canadian Cinema, Television, and Radio Artists)
625 Church Street, 3rd Floor
Toronto, ON M4Y 2G1
(800) 387-3516
(416) 489-1311
e-mail: national@actra.ca
Web site: http://www.actra.com

## Stunt Performers: Life Before the Camera

**Stunts Canada**
2323 Boundary Road, #116
Vancouver, BC V5M 4V8
(604) 299-7050
e-mail: stuntscanada@telus.net
Web site: http://www.stuntscanada.com

# Web Sites

Due to the changing nature of Internet links, the Rosen Publishing Group, Inc., has developed an online list of Web sites related to the subject of this book. This site is updated regularly. Please use this link to access the list:

http://www.rosenlinks.com/ec/stpe

# For Further Reading

Aisbett, Mark. *So You Wanna Be a Stuntman: The Official Stuntman's Guidebook.* Garibaldi Highlands, British Columbia: Lifedrivers, Inc., 1999.

Bucklin, Jack. *Stunt Man: A Freelancer's Guide to Learning the Craft and Landing the Jobs.* Boulder, CO: Paladin Press, 1992.

Canutt, Yakima, and Oliver Drake. *Stunt Man: The Autobiography of Yakima Canutt.* New York: Walker, 1979.

Cherrell, Gwen. *How Movies Are Made.* New York: Facts on File, 1989.

Freese, Gene Scott. *Hollywood Stunt Performers: A Dictionary and Filmography of Over 600 Men and Women, 1922–1996.* Jefferson, NC: McFarland & Co., 1998.

## Stunt Performers: Life Before the Camera

Miklowitz, Gloria D. *Movie Stunts and the People Who Do Them.* New York: Harcourt Brace Jovanovich, 1980.

Stewart, Gail. *Stuntpeople.* Mankato, MN: Crestwood House, 1988.

Sullivan, George, and Tim Sullivan. *Stunt People.* New York: Beaufort Books, 1983.

Weintraub, Aileen. *Stunt Double.* Danbury, CT: Children's Press, 2003.

Wiener, David Jon. *Burns, Falls, and Crashes: Interviews with Movie Stunt Performers.* Jefferson, NC: McFarland & Co., 1996.

# Index

## A
actors/actresses, 5, 6–7, 13–14, 30, 33, 35, 44
Adams, Minerva, 12
agencies and unions, 43–45
air bags, 19
air ram, 30
Aisbett, Mark, 11
Alliance of Canadian Cinema, Television, and Radio Artists (ACTRA), 44
Anderson, Shane "Torch," 5, 22–23
Appleby, James S., 48–49
athleticism, necessity of, 9–11
auditioning, 44

## B
blood, 30, 33–35
breakaway/candy glass, 32
breaking glass/furniture, 30, 32–33, 34
burns, 21–23, 36
*Burns, Falls, and Crashes*, 19, 34, 40
Burson, Polly, 34

## C
Cade, John, 40
car chases/stunt driving, 9, 25–27, 36

# Stunt Performers: Life Before the Camera

Chan, Jackie, 14, 28
computer technology, 34, 41

**D**
danger/dangerous stunts, 5, 8, 11, 12, 16, 21, 24, 42, 51, 53
Davis, Sonja, 16
director, 8, 17, 34, 35, 36, 41, 46, 47
doubling, 5, 7, 13

**E**
explosions, 30, 35

**F**
fear, 11–12, 13, 51
fight scenes, 9, 27–29, 34

**G**
Grace, Martin, 19
gunshots, 30–31

**H**
high falls, 9, 16–19, 36

**I**
injuries, 8, 9, 16, 17, 21, 22, 23, 24, 26–27, 32, 36, 51

**M**
martial arts, 11, 50
meditation/breathing exercises, 12, 51
mental strength, necessity of, 9, 11–12, 50–51
Miklowitz, Gloria D., 34
music videos, 7, 41

**N**
networking, 43
Nomex suits, 21
Norris, Chuck, 14

**O**
Oldenburg, Ann 39

**R**
ratchet, 30–31
rigger, 45–46

**S**
safety measures/protection, 17–19, 21–22, 24, 25–26, 45–46
Screen Actors Guild, 39, 44
second unit director, 46
silent films, 6
Skene, Sean, 42–43
squib, 35

# Index

stunt coordinator, 13, 43, 46
stunt illusions, 29–35
Stuntmen's Association of Motion Pictures, 37, 40, 44
stunt performers
  and acting, 5, 7, 13–14
  and competition, 39–40, 41, 42
  growing demand for, 41
  how they get into the business, 15, 42–43
  requirements for, 9–13, 51
  salaries for, 39–40, 53
stunt performing
  history of, 5–7
  jobs related to, 45–46
stunts, types of, 16–35
sword fights, 5, 6

T

"talkies," 6
transfers, 24

U

United Stuntwomen's Association, 44

V

Van Damme, Jean-Claude, 14
video games, 7, 41
visualization, 12, 51

W

Wiener, David Jon, 34
working well with others, necessity of, 9, 13

**Stunt Performers: Life Before the Camera**

# About the Author

Chérie Turner is an editor and writer who lives in Marin, California.

# Acknowledgments

Thank you to the following stunt performers without whose help this book would not exist: Mark Aisbett, Shane "Torch" Anderson, John Ashker, Melissa Allen, Minerva Adams, and Steven Leavitt.

# Photo Credits

Cover © AP/Wide World Photos; pp. 6, 14, 23, 24–25 © The Everett Collection; p. 10 © Photodisc/Getty Images; pp. 12, 18, 28, 29, 31, 52 courtesy of Lynn Salvatori; p. 17 © Jamie Budge/CORBIS; p. 20 © AP/Wide World Photos; p. 26 © Rick Doyle/Corbis; p. 27 © Rick Doyle/CORBIS; p. 38 © AP Photo World Wide; p. 42 © James P. Blair/Corbis; pp. 44, 50 courtesy of Mike Giansanti.

Thanks to Lynn Salvatori and Mike Giansanti for their time, effort, and personal photos.

Designer: Les Kanturek

www.ingramcontent.com/pod-product-compliance
Lightning Source LLC
Chambersburg PA
CBHW041116070526
44584CB00002B/186